Endorsements

"Co-creation is a dynamic concept that enables people to collaborate in a generative way. Dr. Terry Jackson applies the concept to leadership, and in doing so, he opens up new horizons. *Co-Creation Leadership* opens our eyes to the possibilities of how leaders can build a strong culture capable of achieving sustainable results. Insightful as well as practical, *Co-Creation Leadership* will enable leaders to challenge their assumptions, as well as affirm intentions in order to bring people united in purpose together."
~ John Baldoni, Author of fifteen books, Leadership Educator, Member of Marshall Goldsmith 100 Coaches

"Leadership is a co-creation of the future for all. This is about making a positive difference and revealing people's greatness. In his incredibly practical and wise book, *Co-Creation Leadership*, Dr. Terence Jackson offers a very effective RECIPE model that allows making a leap in performance, whether for underperforming teams or those looking for the next level of success. Dr. Jackson is the master of positive change and this book only proves this."
~ Dr. Oleg Konovalov, Top Global Thought Leader, Best-selling Author of *The Vision Code*, the da Vinci of Visionary Leadership, Member of Marshall Goldsmith 100 Coaches

"Every leader stands to benefit from *Co-Creation Leadership*. Terry serves the need for organizations of all sizes, sectors, or geographies to attend to the basics and bring humanity to the fore of our work. We know that people are the engine of any enterprise, and through his simple RECIPE model, Terry helps you prioritize first things first. Honing the ability to co-create, you learn to make the most of your human assets. This benefits not only organizational performance but also individual satisfaction and connection, creating meaning in being part of a cause bigger than any one of us."
~ Molly Tschang, MBA, Founder of Abella Consulting, Creator of the Say It Skillfully® video series and radio show

"I am honored to endorse Terry Jackson, PhD's latest book, *Co-Creation Leadership*, whose subtitle is 'Helping Leaders Develop Their Superpower of Co-Creation for the Greater Good of the Organization.'

"I have the pleasure of meeting Terry at least once a week. His track record and commitment to making a positive difference in the fields of executive coaching and organizational change are exceptional.

"Terry's desire to help leaders co-create for the greater good is contagious. What I love about *Co-Creation Leadership* is Terry's no-nonsense, common-sense approach and his RECIPE model, which should allow leaders with underperforming teams have a better chance of success, as successful co-creation paves the way for healthier and happier humans, as well as contributes to flourishing organizations that thrive under any circumstance! To conclude, I highly recommend Terry's secret sauce RECIPE, as it will unleash your superpower as a leader of engaged teams, because in today's world, this is of the utmost importance."
~ **Andrew Nowak, Executive Coach, Leadership Development Professional, Member of Marshall Goldsmith 100 Coaches**

"In *Co-Creation Leadership*, Terry Jackson gives us the RECIPE that goes beyond mere collaboration. The greater good of the organization or society is its goal, and it delivers. These leadership insights are the secret sauce to helping us all grow and thrive in uncertain times. A must-read!"
~ **Chester Elton, Best-selling Author of *The Carrot Principle*, *Leading with Gratitude*, and *Anxiety at Work***

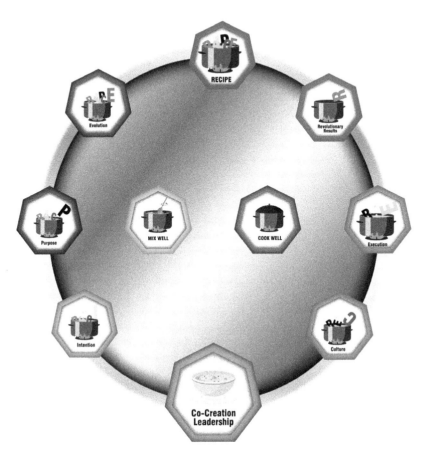

How well is your company executing the Co-Creation RECIPE? Take a 3-minute survey to determine your Co-Creation superpower.
https://aha.pub/CoCreationSurvey

Co-Creation Leadership

Helping Leaders Develop Their Superpower of Co-Creation for the Greater Good of the Organization

Terry Jackson, PhD

Foreword by
Philip M. Brown, Jr., MD

An Actionable Business Journal

E-mail: info@thinkaha.com
20660 Stevens Creek Blvd., Suite 210
Cupertino, CA 95014

Please go to
https://aha.pub/CoCreationLeadership.
to read this AHAbook and to share the
individual AHA messages that resonate with you.

AHAthat

Published by THiNKaha®
20660 Stevens Creek Blvd., Suite 210,
Cupertino, CA 95014
https://thinkaha.com
E-mail: info@thinkaha.com

THiNKaha

First Printing: August 2021
Hardcover ISBN: 978-1-61699-390-0   1-61699-390-1
Paperback ISBN: 978-1-61699-389-4   1-61699-389-8
eBook ISBN: 978-1-61699-388-7   1-61699-388-X
Place of Publication: Silicon Valley, California, USA
Paperback Library of Congress Number: 2021911694

Trademarks

Warning and Disclaimer

Dedication

This book is dedicated to leaders both informal and formal. It is dedicated to those who mentored me without knowing it. It is dedicated to those who came before me whom I admired yet they never knew it. For all of those who served as an example for what to do and for what not to do, I thank you for your guidance.

To all of those whose shoulders I stood on and stand on, I thank you.

Most importantly, this book is dedicated to those who understand that humanity is at its best when it is Co-Creating for the greater good of society and organizations. Our history is full of examples of Co-Creation. We must Co-Create our way to greatness again.

How to Read a THiNKaha® Book

A Note from the Publisher

The AHAthat/THiNKaha series was crafted to deliver content the way humans process information in today's world. Short, sweet, and to the point while delivering powerful, lasting impact.

The content is designed and presented in ways to appeal to visual, auditory, and kinesthetic personality types. Each section contains AHA messages, lines for notes, and a meme that summarizes that section. You should also scan the QR code, or click on the link, to watch a video of the author talking about that section.

This book is contextual in nature. Although the words won't change, their meaning will every time you read it as your context will. Be ready, you will experience your own AHA moments as you read. The AHA messages are designed to be stand-alone actionable messages that will help you think differently. Items to consider as you're reading include:

1. It should only take less than an hour to read the first time. When you're reading, write one to three action items that resonate with you in the underlined areas.

2. Mark your calendar to re-read it again.

3. Repeat step #1 and mark one to three additional AHA messages that resonate. As they will most likely be different, this is a great time to reflect on the messages that resonated with you during your last reading.

4. Sprinkle credust on the author and yourself by sharing the AHA messages from this book socially from the AHAthat platform https://aha.pub/CoCreationLeadership.

After reading this THiNKaha book, marking your AHA messages, rereading it, and marking more AHA messages, you'll begin to see how this book contextually applies to you. We advocate for continuous, lifelong learning and this book will help you transform your AHAs into action items with tangible results.

Mitchell Levy, Global Credibility Expert
publisher@thinkaha.com

A THiNKaha book is not your typical book. It's a whole lot more, while being a whole lot less. Scan the QR code or use this link to watch me talk about this new evolutionary style of book: https://aha.pub/THiNKahaSeries

Contents

Foreword

The competitive landscape has been forever changed by the events related to and temporally associated with the global COVID-19 pandemic. We find ourselves in an environment that none of us has ever navigated, even if parts of it presently appear familiar. The underlying truth is that nothing is as clear to each of us as it was even a single year ago, and our "go-to methods" of driving results can put us at career and business risk at unprecedented rates.

Much of what we have long believed was history is proving to be a fantasy, and while there are opportunities for increasing clarity around the factors that have led us to this moment in time, never has there been such a combination of ambiguity and information overload acting in concert to make decision-making such a perilous process. Our individual interpretations are remarkably incomplete representations of fact, and one person's truth has some level of vague overlap with that of another. As a result, the best path forward is unclear at best, as our gaps in understanding immovable forces may lead us to many false starts, wasted efforts, and futile attempts to create the next generation of processes and products that further our society and our world.

So, the simple truth is that we all need help to clarify the best opportunities for breakthrough results. No single person has the best answers or the elusive "recipe for success" that becomes the holy grail for successfully navigating the proverbial quest for success.

Enter Dr. Terence Jackson. While so many seem to persist in the search for some successful RECIPE that once and for all provides the clear path to outstanding results, thereby revolutionizing the way that we work and think, Terry courageously fills that space with the idea that it doesn't work that way. His RECIPE is much different, acknowledging the rapidly changing dynamics and suggesting a different path forward that pays homage to the adage, "To go fast, go alone. To go far, go together."

So, if you seek a source that provides a method to navigate, a means to again find the way forward to produce outcomes that have a chance of being truly remarkable and perhaps exponential, Terry's book, *Co-Creation Leadership*, is definitely for you. He acknowledges the complexity of our true current environment and reveals pathways that provide the opportunity to draw out the best ideas time and again, paving the path to collaboratively created revolutionary results. I hope that you find it as enlightening as I have.

Philip M. Brown, Jr., MD
Novant Health Chief Community Impact Officer

Introduction

The COVID-19 global pandemic has revealed the fragility of humanity. Uncertainty and ambiguity are the ways of the world today, so leaders must adapt and rise to the challenge. In this environment, co-creation leadership is a superpower that leaders need in order to help their organizations thrive.

Co-creation is when two or more people collaborate to achieve a common goal. Co-creation leadership can bring people together to generate success for the greater good of the organization.

In this book, Dr. Terry Jackson, a renowned expert in executive coaching and organizational change, discusses how all leaders can use co-creation leadership to achieve success in any organization—whether an independent business, a publicly-traded company, a nonprofit foundation, a church group, or a board of directors. He also introduces the co-creation leadership's RECIPE model:

(R) Revolutionary Results.
Co-creation leadership can produce *revolutionary results* because co-creation is, in and of itself, a revolution. Leaders need to ensure that their co-creation isn't merely lip service; otherwise, real transformation can't take place.

(E) Execution.
Leaders should *execute* the plans and initiatives to help the organization produce better solutions for their customers. Just imagine what humans could do if they never heard the words "failure" and "limitation."

(C) Culture.
The *culture* set by co-creation leadership is all about the "why." It serves as the North Star for any person in the organization. Co-creation leadership can help create a healthy culture with fully engaged employees, improved performance, and increased productivity.

(I) Intention.

Co-creation leadership is intentional leadership. Leaders should intentionally develop those in the organization to their fullest potential and encourage them to collaborate for the company's greater good.

(P) Purpose.

Purpose is a key part of co-creation leadership because it allows leaders and those in the organization to continually want to grow and succeed. Co-creation leadership helps people live their purpose, resulting in increased intent and motivation to succeed.

(E) Evolution.

A thriving organization is a constantly evolving organization. *Evolution* is all about growth and transformation. Co-creation leadership pushes everyone in the organization to explore new possibilities and embrace transformation in order to succeed.

All six components in co-creation leadership—revolutionary results, execution, culture, intention, purpose, and evolution—are equally important in building a co-creative organization. Take one element away, and the RECIPE of co-creation leadership is incomplete.

Leaders with underperforming teams can recognize and apply the components in co-creation to have a better chance of success. Successful co-creation paves the way for healthier and happier humans and contributes to flourishing and thriving organizations.

Share the AHA messages from this book socially by going to
https://aha.pub/CoCreationLeadership.

*Scan the QR code or use this link to watch the
section videos and more on this section topic:*
https://aha.pub/CoCreationLeadershipSVs

Section I

Why Is Co-Creation Leadership a Must in Today's World?

The COVID-19 pandemic has revealed the fragility of humanity. Leaders today need to step up and navigate uncertainty and ambiguity in order to build thriving organizations. This is where the superpower of co-creation leadership comes in.

Any leadership role is a privilege. It's an art and a science that involves learning new things and creating an environment for organizations to excel. Co-creation becomes a part of the organizational DNA when there is a rhythm that ties into people's emotions to take action to achieve a common goal.

Co-creation leadership is a superpower that is greatly needed today.

The co-creation process promotes a sense of shared ownership and excitement within an organization. It brings new voices and ideas into the fold. When leaders open up to suggestions and are willing to consider each on its own merit, they can come up with solutions beneficial to the whole organization.

With co-creation leadership, members of the organization develop greater loyalty. This is because co-creation stimulates positive interaction, which results in a workplace where everyone is valued.

Co-creation allows everyone to bring something to the table despite differences in perspectives, experience, and skill. A great sense of collaboration is encouraged to surpass challenges and obstacles together.

This section talks about the importance of co-creation leadership, especially during difficult times, like the COVID-19 global pandemic, when the world faced significant changes and disruptions. When the workplace and workforce change, co-creation leadership becomes more relevant in understanding the intersection of instinct and intellect in leading organizations to success.

1

Bringing together people's knowledge bases, experiences, and perspectives can mobilize efforts to advance any organization's goal. #CoCreationLeadership

_____

_____

_____

2

Co-creation is humanity at its best. It's all about working hand-in-hand for the greater good of each society, each other, and the organization. #CoCreationLeadership

_____

_____

_____

3

Co-creation is the secret sauce that differentiates
excellence from success. Success is too often
transactional and excellence is systemic.
#CoCreationLeadership

_____

_____

_____

4

No man is an island. Co-creation produces better results
than individual efforts. #CoCreationLeadership

_____

_____

_____

5

Co-creation is caring as much about your fellow humans' success as your own. It's a superpower that not everyone has, but it can be learned. #CoCreationLeadership

_____

_____

6

Co-creation is the process of appealing to the hearts and minds of others for the greater good. #CoCreationLeadership

_____

_____

_____

7

Companies today seek help with communication
and collaboration because many people lack these
soft skills that play a huge part in co-creation.
#CoCreationLeadership

_____

_____

_____

8

Successful corporations experience an internal rhythm
in their co-creation that other companies don't. This
rhythm is tied to the emotions of those who are working
toward a common goal. #CoCreationLeadership

_____

_____

_____

9

Co-creation is the ability to sell an idea to others so they might become part of something bigger than themselves. #CoCreationLeadership

_____

_____

_____

10

Leaders who can remove ambiguity and uncertainty from their objectives understand #CoCreationLeadership.

_____

_____

_____

11

Humans are naturally drawn to co-create when they find a compelling reason to buy into the shared vision and objective. #CoCreationLeadership

_____

_____

_____

12

The best leaders mobilize their teams by uniting them around a shared vision and a common goal. Do you? #CoCreationLeadership

_____

_____

_____

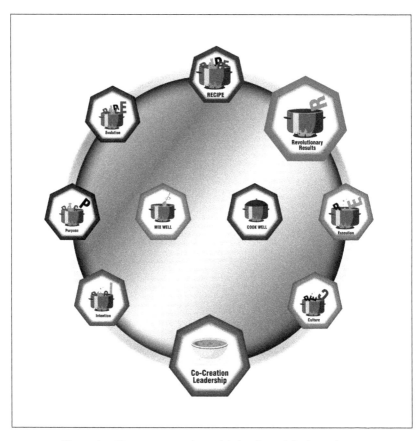

Share the AHA messages from this book socially by going to
https://aha.pub/CoCreationLeadership.

Scan the QR code or use this link to watch the section videos and more on this section topic:
https://aha.pub/CoCreationLeadershipSVs

Section II

Revolutionary Results

Nowadays, optimal results no longer cut it. For a business to thrive, especially during unprecedented times like the COVID-19 global pandemic, leaders need unprecedented ways of doing business.

Co-creation leadership is a commitment not only to results but also to *revolutionary* results.

When co-creation leaders invest in people, it creates more jobs, more opportunities, and more growth with unimaginable exploits!

Co-creation is, in and of itself, a revolution and one that requires transformational leadership. Therefore, co-creation leadership must not merely pay lip service to the underlying work; otherwise, real transformation cannot take place.

Organizational leaders who continue to push boundaries and challenge the status quo are the ones who survive, thrive, and achieve revolutionary results.

This section shows leaders how every possible business initiative (e.g., diversity and inclusion, growth alignment, and succession planning) can achieve revolutionary results with co-creation.

13

These are unprecedented times due to the many dynamics in society. Social justice issues have heightened the division of humanity. Learning, implementing, and executing #CoCreationLeadership help resolve these divides.

_____

_____

_____

14

Leaders can transform complex problems into clearly defined solutions with #CoCreationLeadership.

_____

_____

_____

15

Truly understanding the needs of society will help create solutions for the greater good. This mindset produces revolutionary results. #CoCreationLeadership

_____

_____

_____

16

Start with the end in mind — this is a fundamental philosophy in life. Envisioning the desired outcome helps leaders achieve revolutionary results. #CoCreationLeadership

_____

_____

_____

17

Great leaders are those who want revolutionary results. They maximize opportunities to pursue organizational growth. #CoCreationLeadership

_____

_____

_____

18

#CoCreationLeadership is value-based leadership. To achieve revolutionary results, you need more than lip service.

_____

_____

_____

19

Transformational leaders understand that every business initiative can be visualized and improved through #CoCreationLeadership.

_____

_____

_____

20

Transformational leaders have disruptive mindsets. They create something new and produce revolutionary results. #CoCreationLeadership

---

21

Revolutionary results are expected from transformational leaders. When hearts and minds are attuned to a common goal for the greater good, that's co-creation. #CoCreationLeadership

---

22

When an organization adapts #CoCreationLeadership
and invests in its people, it can create more jobs,
opportunities, and growth.

_____

_____

_____

23

Organizations can unlock revolutionary results when
they invest in people, society, and technology through
#CoCreationLeadership.

_____

_____

_____

24

There must be a "we" in our hearts and minds to end prejudices that cause division. Revolutionary results happen when real transformation takes place. #CoCreationLeadership

_____

_____

_____

25

Organizations that know how to co-create are the ones that succeed and achieve revolutionary results. #CoCreationLeadership

_____

_____

_____

26

Organizations and people thrive when they push through boundaries to achieve revolutionary results.
#CoCreationLeadership

_____

_____

_____

27

#CoCreationLeadership produces revolutionary results.

_____

_____

_____

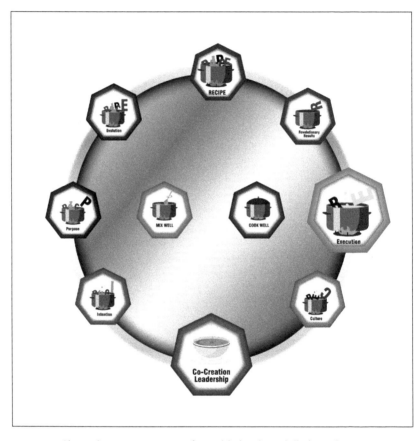

Share the AHA messages from this book socially by going to
https://aha.pub/CoCreationLeadership.

Scan the QR code or use this link to watch the section videos and more on this section topic: https://aha.pub/CoCreationLeadershipSVs

Section III

Execution

Co-creation leadership is all about making things happen.

**Ideas are worth nothing without *execution*,
no matter how smart they might sound.**

Successful leaders need more than strategy—they need active execution and follow-through. The execution component of co-creation leadership involves treating your business strategy not as a one-and-done document, but as a living, breathing entity that evolves in real time. You will be able to course-correct more accurately and with better results when you revisit, re-analyze, and routinely update your execution plan.

Having a growth mindset is key for leaders to better execute strategies and plans. When leaders are not stuck by growth-stopping words like "failure" and "limitation," they can find solutions to take the business to the next level.

Execution boils down to accountability. Great leaders hold themselves accountable and ask the same for everyone else in the organization. They place the same standards on all levels—no hierarchy or seniority excused. The accountability factor embedded in co-creation keeps things in check to make sure there's no misalignment.

Successful execution happens when people work toward the same goals. A team that encourages collaboration and trust can bring something transformational to the table. With co-creation leadership, everyone in the organization contributes to the successful execution of its strategy.

This section covers how leaders can successfully execute company strategies and plans with co-creation leadership. This includes the importance of promoting a growth mindset, accountability, collaboration, trust, and teamwork for the business to thrive.

28

Execution is making things happen. Co-creation is successful when leaders execute a strategy with their people. #CoCreationLeadership

---

29

One of the challenges the corporate world faces is the inability to execute. Reasons include hidden agendas, misalignment, and lack of engagement. #CoCreationLeadership

---

30

Successful leaders need more than strategy;
they need active execution and follow-through.
#CoCreationLeadership

_____

_____

_____

31

Successful leaders execute plans and initiatives to
help the organization produce better solutions for their
customers.

_____

_____

_____

32

Saying one thing and doing another is a sign of poor execution and poor leadership. #CoCreationLeadership

_____

_____

_____

33

Execution involves treating your business strategy not as a one-and-done document, but as a living, breathing entity that evolves over time. #CoCreationLeadership

_____

_____

_____

34

Leaders with a growth mindset are willing to execute plans and find solutions to take the business to the next level. #CoCreationLeadership

_____

_____

_____

35

Leaders who disavow words like "failure" and "limitation" execute better. Imagine what you could achieve if you never heard those words. #GrowthMindset #CoCreationLeadership

_____

_____

_____

36

Leaders should maintain a growth mindset for better execution. #CoCreationLeadership means providing opportunities for people to improve their skills.

_____

_____

_____

37

Execution boils down to accountability. Co-creation has accountability embedded into the organization's culture, so leaders are naturally steered toward action. #CoCreationLeadership

_____

_____

_____

38

Successful leaders are those who hold themselves and everyone else in the organization accountable. #CoCreationLeadership.

_____

_____

_____

39

Personal accountability is important in #CoCreationLeadership. It means you're accountable for the job you do in helping the company succeed.

_____

_____

_____

40

Peer accountability is important in #CoCreationLeadership. When peers hold each other accountable, they can improve beyond perceived personal limitations.

_____

_____

_____

41

Successful execution happens when people work toward the same goals. #CoCreationLeadership

_____

_____

_____

42

Execution takes a village, not a single leader. Everyone must participate in co-creation to achieve lasting impacts for the greater good. #CoCreationLeadership

---

43

Agility, collaboration, trust, and teamwork are essential in executing successful strategies. #CoCreationLeadership

---

44

Teams need trust to drive growth in business. #CoCreationLeadership is about trust, which is essential to execution.

_____

_____

_____

45

Everyone can contribute when every voice is heard. That's #CoCreationLeadership, which leads to effective execution.

_____

_____

_____

46

#CoCreationLeadership is about the team. For execution to be effective, organizations must move away from "I" and think as one.

_____

_____

_____

47

When everyone in the organization makes critical contributions, it's easier to execute strategies for the company's greater good. #CoCreationLeadership

_____

_____

_____

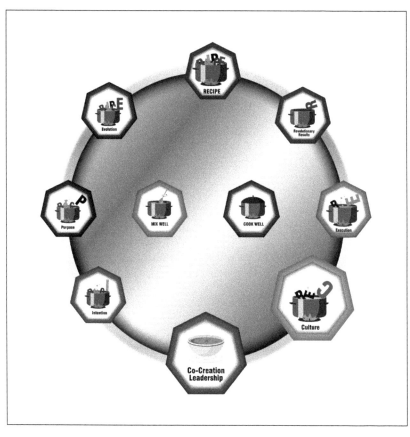

Share the AHA messages from this book socially by going to
https://aha.pub/CoCreationLeadership.

Scan the QR code or use this link to watch the section videos and more on this section topic:
https://aha.pub/CoCreationLeadershipSVs

Section IV

Culture

Leaders who want a thriving organization need to think of culture.

The *culture* set by co-creation leadership is all about the "why" because co-creation is about people, and people seek purpose.

Co-creation is a movement; this means people need to be on the same page to co-create effectively. The collective hearts and minds of those in the organization need to be aligned. This can be achieved by having a healthy culture.

The organizational culture is largely a reflection of its leaders. It plays a significant role in the productivity of teams. That's why leaders need to create a "listening and executing" culture to bring out the best in their teams.

A good organizational culture is one where trust is the predominant energy. Trust is cultivated with the utmost care and respect. Good communication between leaders and their teams also results in getting support and genuine engagement.

Co-creation leaders can help drive high team performance, which contributes to the organization's success. They can help create a healthy culture with fully engaged employees, improved performance, and increased productivity.

This section covers the humanity involved in a co-creative organization, where imperfect people can show vulnerability and still progress by learning from and supporting one another at all costs.

48

Co-creation is a movement. The collective hearts and minds of those in the organization need to be aligned in order to co-create effectively. #Culture #CoCreationLeadership

_____

_____

_____

49

The culture set by #CoCreationLeadership is all about the "why." The "why" serves as the team's North Star because co-creation is about people, and people seek purpose.

_____

_____

_____

50

A co-creational leader's belief system trickles down not only to inspire and motivate the team, but also to enroll them in the purpose. If the leader's purpose is to serve, the challenge is, "How can you serve?" #CoCreationLeadership

_____

_____

_____

51

Hearts and minds are drawn to good, effective leadership. #CoCreationLeadership is a magnet for people who want to contribute for the success of the business.

_____

_____

_____

52

The culture of #CoCreationLeadership includes outstanding communication. A sign of a strong leader is the ability to communicate well and avoid misunderstanding.

53

Leaders can only execute at the level of their ability to listen. Creating a "listening and executing" culture can help build trust and take the business to new heights. #CoCreationLeadership

54

When leaders take time to listen, people feel wanted,
seen, and understood. #CoCreationLeadership

_____

_____

_____

55

The culture created by #CoCreationLeadership calls for
people to support one another for the good of all.

_____

_____

_____

56

Successful organizations have a culture that encourages creativity and innovation. #CoCreationLeadership

_____

_____

_____

57

A culture that encourages creativity and innovation is set when leaders focus on honing individual talents and igniting creativity in the team. #CoCreationLeadership

_____

_____

_____

58

Successful organizations have leaders who are comfortable challenging the status quo and willing to take risks. #CoCreationLeadership

_____

_____

_____

59

Good leaders are calculated risk-takers who manage risk well. The culture set by #CoCreationLeadership is not risk-averse.

_____

_____

_____

60

Perpetual recalibration and alignment on a day-to-day basis should be part of an organization's culture.
#CoCreationLeadership

_____

_____

_____

61

Productive teams cultivate a mindset of doing things right the first time. This also means being open to changes and learning from mistakes.
#CoCreationLeadership

_____

_____

_____

62

Organizations with a good culture have people who are emotionally invested. Emotionally invested individuals actively contribute to the success of the business. #CoCreationLeadership

_____

_____

_____

63

#CoCreationLeadership helps create a healthy culture with fully engaged employees, improved performance, and increased productivity.

_____

_____

_____

64

Co-creation is not about position, role, or title. It is about a purposeful contribution by all in the process of co-creating a future where all thrive. #CoCreationLeadership

_____

_____

_____

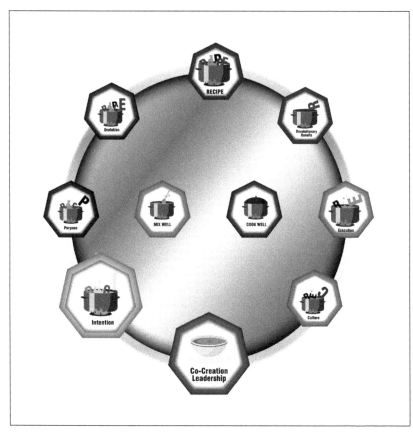

Share the AHA messages from this book socially by going to
https://aha.pub/CoCreationLeadership.

Scan the QR code or use this link to watch the section videos and more on this section topic:
https://aha.pub/CoCreationLeadershipSVs

Section V

Intention

Leaders must lead by example. When leaders are seen intentionally being of service to others, everyone in the organization is likely to respect and follow their lead.

Co-creation leaders who always model quality and excellence set their *intention* for the rest of the team to follow.

Co-creation leadership is intentional leadership—it puts the organization's agenda before any individual agenda. It's all about the leader's intention to develop people to their fullest potential and encourage them to collaborate for the betterment of the company.

Being intentional in co-creation leadership requires courage and accountability, and it shows the desire to create a meaningful impact throughout the organization.

This section discusses the impact of leaders who intend to lead their members and the organization to success. With co-creation leadership, the whole organization will be *intent* on producing desired results. Not only does that drive growth and profit for the company, but it also provides a better quality of life for those in it.

When co-creation leaders show their intention to build a thriving organization, so will everyone else in the organization. When people are *intent* on thriving, the company *will* thrive.

65

#CoCreationLeadership is about being intentional in serving and leading people toward personal and organizational success. #LeadIntentionally

---

66

Being intentional is the beginning of any transformation that a person, organization, or company wants to make. #LeadIntentionally #CoCreationLeadership

---

67

Intention is the foundation of transformation. New perspectives can make things happen when certain mental models are deconstructed. #LeadIntentionally #CoCreationLeadership

---

68

Everyone in the organization is human. Unclear intentions create barriers that stop humans from understanding and respecting one another. #LeadIntentionally #CoCreationLeadership

---

69

Leaders who are clear with their intentions have a better chance of being understood and respected than those who aren't. #LeadIntentionally #CoCreationLeadership

---

70

Can a leader positively impact the organization by showing their intentions? Yes! Leaders are more likely to be respected and followed when they do. #LeadIntentionally #CoCreationLeadership

---

71

Execution is transforming intention into reality.
Therefore, it's important to understand what
the leaders' intentions are. #LeadIntentionally
#CoCreationLeadership

_____

_____

_____

72

Leaders can demonstrate their intentions through their
thoughts, actions, and responses. #LeadIntentionally
#CoCreationLeadership

_____

_____

_____

73

When you consider every decision that a successful leader makes, it should become clear that their intention is in the right place. #LeadIntentionally #CoCreationLeadership

---

74

Leaders should think about the impact of every choice they make. How do their choices affect the greater good? #LeadIntentionally #CoCreationLeadership

---

75

Courage and accountability are key tenets of revolutionary change that is brought about with #CoCreationLeadership. Without it, success can't happen. #LeadIntentionally

---

76

When leaders are accountable alongside everyone else, it demonstrates courage and intentional leadership. #LeadIntentionally #CoCreationLeadership

---

77

Leaders should work to empower everyone in the organization to be courageous in their pursuit of success. #LeadIntentionally #CoCreationLeadership

---

78

The team's goals and objectives — not any single person's — are the guiding forces in intentional leadership. #LeadIntentionally #CoCreationLeadership

---

79

Being intentional in #CoCreationLeadership involves having every employee working together to serve one another in reaching a common goal. #LeadIntentionally

_____

_____

_____

80

Co-creation is never about the title that one can attain. It's about working together and rallying everyone in the organization around a common purpose. #LeadIntentionally #CoCreationLeadership

_____

_____

_____

81

The intention of any company shouldn't just be about profits or growth. It should also be about making people's lives better. #LeadIntentionally #CoCreationLeadership

_____

_____

_____

82

#CoCreationLeadership works if the intention revolves around being of service to others. #LeadIntentionally

_____

_____

_____

83

#CoCreationLeadership sets a culture within the organization that is intentional about being of service, whether it is to workmates or clients.

_____

_____

_____

84

With #CoCreationLeadership, organization members will be intent on producing desired results. #LeadIntentionally

_____

_____

_____

85

Capacity and capability are two different things. If a leader's intention is to add capability but not expand capacity, their efforts are futile. #LeadIntentionally #CoCreationLeadership

_____

_____

_____

86

Leaders can encourage the team to be intentional. Likewise, the team can — and should — encourage the leader. #LeadIntentionally #CoCreationLeadership

_____

_____

_____

87

When co-creation leaders show their intention to thrive, so will everyone else in the organization. When people are intent on thriving, the company will thrive. #LeadIntentionally #CoCreationLeadership

---

88

The intention of #CoCreationLeadership is to develop human beings to their fullest potential for their own betterment and for that of the organization.

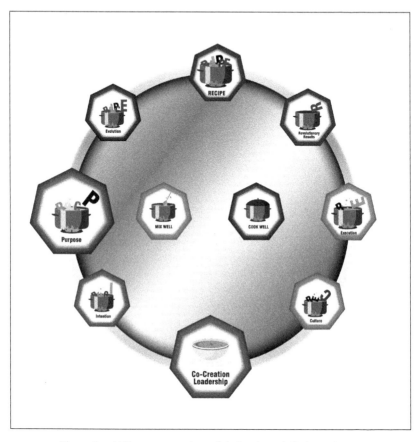

Share the AHA messages from this book socially by going to
https://aha.pub/CoCreationLeadership.

*Scan the QR code or use this link to watch the
section videos and more on this section topic:*
https://aha.pub/CoCreationLeadershipSVs

Section VI

Purpose

Purpose is a crucial part of co-creation leadership, as it allows leaders and those in the organization to continually want to grow and succeed.

**What leaders and individuals in an organization do is
only ever as good as why they do it—their *purpose*.**

Purpose is the "why" behind a human being's existence. Living a life without purpose is like driving a car without knowing where to go.

Co-creation leaders help those in their organizations find and live their purpose. They understand that purpose motivates those in the organization to make an impact in the work they do.

When a person's purpose is fueled by passion (i.e., what they love to do), they can go beyond their normal capacities and achieve unimaginable things, both personally and professionally. Co-creation leadership promotes this, resulting in an organization that thrives and succeeds.

Co-creation leadership supports those who will give their all to build an organization that serves its purpose, not only for the business but also for the betterment of society and humanity. When individual and corporate purpose align inner fulfillment and success can be achieved.

This section covers how co-creation leaders can lead purposefully and enable those in their organizations to live and work purposefully to deliver great results that make a difference.

89

Co-creation leaders deliver great results, and they do so
by helping those in the organization feel connected
to the company's purpose. #CoCreationLeadership

_____

_____

_____

90

When the purpose of an organization and its employees
are aligned, it creates higher levels of motivation and
engagement. #CoCreationLeadership

_____

_____

_____

91

#CoCreationLeadership depends on everyone contributing. If everyone's purpose is to help innovate or co-create, the organization can achieve success.

_____

_____

_____

92

#CoCreationLeadership acknowledges that everyone can contribute. Everyone can help innovate and co-create. #Purpose

_____

_____

_____

93

Sometimes there is no problem to solve, only a new process to discover that makes things better and simpler. #Purpose enabled by #CoCreationLeadership motivates those in the organization to contribute.

94

Having a purpose allows people in the organization to continually want to grow and succeed together. #CoCreationLeadership

---

95

#CoCreationLeadership provides the opportunity
for people to fulfill their #Purpose.

_____

_____

_____

96

Leaders can help those in the organization find their
#Purpose and live it through #CoCreationLeadership.

_____

_____

_____

97

When the purpose is clear, it's easier for people to co-create and find smart solutions. #CoCreationLeadership

_____

_____

_____

98

The purpose of an organization (i.e., the "why") can bring everyone together and move toward a common goal. #CoCreationLeadership

_____

_____

_____

99

If those in the organization have an idea of their life purpose, a co-creation leader should encourage them to build on that. #CoCreationLeadership is about developing people's potential.

_____

_____

_____

100

#Purpose boosts people's capacity to make the greatest impact in the work they do. #CoCreationLeadership

_____

_____

_____

101

Growth rarely happens inside the comfort zone. Learning to be uncomfortable stretches limits and helps people find their #Purpose. #CoCreationLeadership

_____

_____

_____

102

#Purpose, which is fueled by passion, propels people in the organization to thrive. #CoCreationLeadership

_____

_____

_____

103

Passion is what people love doing. If the passion of those in the organization fuels their #Purpose, they become more driven to succeed. #CoCreationLeadership

_____

_____

_____

104

#Purpose is the "why" behind a human being's existence. It's a key part of #CoCreationLeadership.

_____

_____

_____

105

What leaders and individuals in an organization do is only ever as good as why they do it. #Purpose #CoCreationLeadership

_____

_____

_____

106

Living a life without #Purpose is like driving a racecar without knowing where the finish line is. #CoCreationLeadership

_____

_____

_____

107

The emotional factor involved with having a #Purpose in life can help people achieve unimaginable things personally and professionally. #CoCreationLeadership

_____

_____

_____

108

When those in the organization feel like they are living their #Purpose, they are more likely to increase their intent to perform at a higher level. #CoCreationLeadership

_____

_____

_____

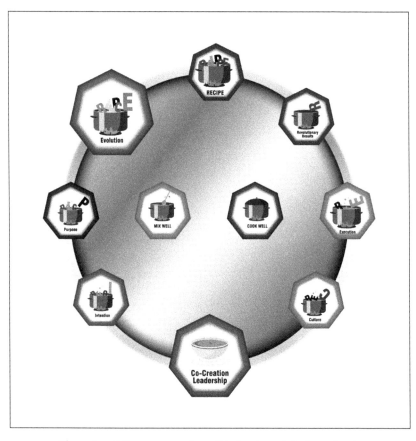

Share the AHA messages from this book socially by going to
https://aha.pub/CoCreationLeadership.

Scan the QR code or use this link to watch the section videos and more on this section topic:
https://aha.pub/CoCreationLeadershipSVs

Section VII

Evolution

Evolution is all about exploring possibilities. When organization members explore possibilities through co-creation leadership, transformation happens.

It's not the biggest or most intelligent companies that thrive and succeed; it's the ones that constantly *evolve*.

Co-creation leadership encourages evolution for the organization to grow, transform, and succeed. Co-creation leaders nurture people within the organization. They help them discover their capacities and strengths and provide them with the support that they need to reach the next level. When people within the organization evolve, the whole organization does too.

By encouraging evolution, co-creation leadership pushes those in the organization to explore new possibilities and embrace transformation. Exploring possibilities can lead to discovering how the organization can go where it needs to be.

Evolution is about shaking, disrupting, and rebuilding the status quo. It involves constantly challenging old ways of thinking to make way for a better future, not only for the individual but also for the whole organization.

This section covers how co-creation leaders should encourage evolution within the organization. Empowering people to evolve can lead to a continually growing, transforming, and thriving organization.

109

A thriving organization is a constantly evolving organization. #CoCreationLeadership encourages evolution in order for the organization to grow, transform, and succeed.

_____

_____

_____

110

#CoCreationLeadership nurtures people to their highest potential, understands their capacities, and helps them reach the next level. That's how an organization evolves.

_____

_____

_____

111

Organizations that shy away from evolution run the risk of limiting their own growth. #CoCreationLeadership takes time.

_____

_____

_____

112

Growth is a key factor of a thriving organization. #CoCreationLeadership encourages evolution for the growth of those in the organization.

_____

_____

_____

113

By encouraging evolution, #CoCreationLeadership pushes everyone in the organization to explore new possibilities and embrace transformation.

_____

_____

_____

114

Exploration and evolution are continuing processes in #CoCreationLeadership. A great deal of courage and curiosity is involved in exploring possibilities.

_____

_____

_____

115

No stone is left unturned in exploring possibilities.
#CoCreationLeadership involves copious amounts of
thinking, doing, and repurposing.

116

The process of improvement within an organization
opens doors to exploring the possibilities of
#CoCreationLeadership.

117

Organizations must explore opportunities to improve work processes. Leaders should continue to tweak the structure to get the organization where it needs to be. #CoCreationLeadership.

_____

_____

_____

118

Evolution is transformation. Transforming means creating something new, which is essential in #CoCreationLeadership.

_____

_____

_____

119

Evolution through transformation means putting things in place that could benefit everyone. #CoCreationLeadership

_____

_____

_____

120

Evolution enabled by #CoCreationLeadership produces products and services that revolutionize markets.

_____

_____

_____

121

At the heart of co-creation is everyone's voice being heard. This is the evolution of a corporation from simple leadership to #CoCreationLeadership.

_____

_____

_____

122

In order to succeed, co-creators ask, "Where do we want to be?" They recognize what's changing in the external environment. #CoCreationLeadership

_____

_____

_____

123

Evolution is always about shaking things up
and rebuilding. #CoCreationLeadership

_____

_____

_____

124

To evolve, old ways of thinking are challenged to make
way for better solutions. #CoCreationLeadership
is about non-traditional thought processes.

_____

_____

_____

125

#CoCreationLeadership means empowering people to co-create solutions that help improve society. These solutions make way for the evolution of humankind.

_____

_____

_____

126

#CoCreationLeadership pushes everyone in the organization to explore new possibilities, encourage evolution, and embrace transformation in order to succeed.

_____

_____

_____

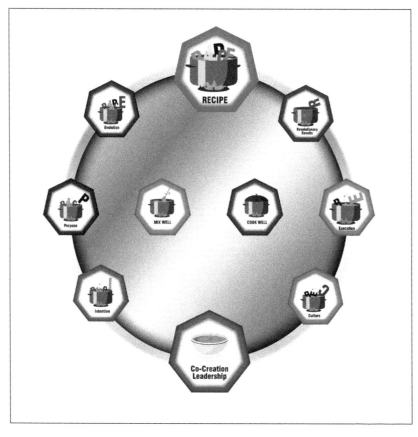

Share the AHA messages from this book socially by going to
https://aha.pub/CoCreationLeadership.

Scan the QR code or use this link to watch the
section videos and more on this section topic:
https://aha.pub/CoCreationLeadershipSVs

Section VIII

Conclusion

Co-creation leadership is a superpower that can help individuals, organizations, and humanity thrive. It enables those in the organization to move forward even amid uncertainty or instability.

Leaders who want to build and sustain a high-performing team and a thriving organization should understand that co-creation is the answer.

With the RECIPE model, leaders can easily align their teams to co-create and succeed together.

All six components of the co-creation leadership RECIPE—revolutionary results, execution, culture, intention, purpose, and evolution—are equally important in building a co-creative organization.

As businesses create solutions that bring in billions of dollars of profit, the ultimate reward is how successful organizations can benefit the greater good. They do this by providing people with a chance to be part of organizations that transform other people's lives, not just their own.

Co-creation leadership is not about getting those in the organization to follow you toward the future; it's about getting them to co-create the future with you.

Co-creation leadership is all about creating an environment for those in the organization to excel and bring about the organization's success. Co-creation leadership is a key success factor in creating and sustaining a thriving organization.

127

#CoCreationLeadership is a superpower that can help individuals, organizations, and humanity thrive.

_____

_____

_____

128

#CoCreationLeadership helps organizations flourish and thrive under any circumstances.

_____

_____

_____

129

#CoCreationLeadership is a higher purpose that requires higher expectations. Co-creation leaders who want to help organizations thrive and succeed must go above and beyond what is required.

_____

_____

_____

130

Leaders should not just use their personal experiences or the same leadership recipes over and over again. They need #CoCreationLeadership.

_____

_____

_____

131

#CoCreationLeadership has a RECIPE that will bring out the superpowers that an organization needs to thrive.

132

The #CoCreationLeadership RECIPE model (revolutionary results, execution, culture, intention, purpose, and evolution) enables leaders and organizations to navigate new frontiers.

133

Leaders need to incorporate the #CoCreationLeadership RECIPE model (revolutionary results, execution, culture, intention, purpose, and evolution) in their day-to-day operations to build a co-creative organization successfully.

134

Just like in cooking, the ingredients in the #CoCreationLeadership RECIPE (revolutionary results, execution, culture, intention, purpose, and evolution) are equally important to create a great dish.

135

A thriving organization is one where there's alignment in the RECIPE (revolutionary results, execution, culture, intention, purpose, and evolution).
Leaders who cook this way create tasty meals.

_____

_____

_____

136

We have been sold on individualism when co-creation is the answer to build and sustain a thriving organization.
#CoCreationLeadership

_____

_____

_____

137

Revolutionary results are not achieved by a single person in the organization. They are achieved when everyone in the organization co-creates.
#CoCreationLeadership

_____

_____

_____

138

Neale Donald Walsch says, "The era of the single savior is over. What is needed now is joint action, combined effort, and collective co-creation." #CoCreationLeadership

_____

_____

_____

139

Co-creation leaders are not necessarily those who have the greatest accomplishments. They are the driving forces that get those in the organization to achieve those accomplishments. #CoCreationLeadership

_____

_____

_____

140

#CoCreationLeadership is not about getting those in the organization to follow you toward the future; it's about getting them to co-create the future with you.

_____

_____

_____

About the Author

Dr. Terry Jackson is a dynamic executive advisor, thought leader, TEDx speaker, and organizational consultant. He is a member of the prestigious Marshall Goldsmith 100 Coaches and was recently chosen by Thinkers50 as one of the Top 50 Leaders in Executive Coaching. Terry was named by Thinkers360 as a Top 20 Global Leader in the Future of Work, while *CIO Review* magazine named his consulting company, JCG Consulting Group LLC, one of the Top 10 Most Promising Leadership Development Solution Providers in 2019. He earned a PhD in management, with a concentration in leadership and organizational change. He is the author of the book, *Transformational Thinking: The First Step toward Individual and Organizational Greatness*. He has also contributed to articles in *Forbes* and *Chief Executive* magazine and has authored more than 150 articles on LinkedIn.

Terry has served as a business coach for startups and coached executives at ExxonMobil, Norfolk Southern Corp, Valassis, DellEMC, New York Life, Pakistan government, Amazon, McDonald's, New Hanover Regional Medical Center, InOutsource Consulting Group, IBM, Howard University, and Connected Investors.

THiNKaha has created AHAthat for you to share content from this book.

- Share each AHA message socially: **https://aha.pub/CoCreationLeadership.**
- Share additional content: **https://AHAthat.com**
- Info on authoring: **https://AHAthat.com/Author**

CPSIA information can be obtained
at www.ICGtesting.com
Printed in the USA
BVHW052029080821
613785BV00004B/93

9 781616 993894